W9-ATT-375

STERLING CHILDREN'S BOOKS
New York

An Imprint of Sterling Publishing Co., Inc.
1166 Avenue of the Americas
New York, NY 10036

STERLING CHILDREN'S BOOK and the distinctive Sterling Children's Books logo
are registered trademarks of Sterling Publishing Co., Inc.

Text © 2019 Mary Kay Carson

All rights reserved. No part of this publication may be reproduced, stored in a retrieval system,
or transmitted in any form or by any means (including electronic, mechanical, photocopying,
recording, or otherwise) without prior written permission from the publisher.

ISBN 978-1-4549-2967-3

Distributed in Canada by Sterling Publishing Co., Inc.
C/o Canadian Manda Group, 664 Annette Street
Toronto, Ontario M6S 2C8, Canada
Distributed in the United Kingdom by GMC Distribution Services
Castle Place, 166 High Street, Lewes, East Sussex BN7 1XU, England
Distributed in Australia by NewSouth Books
45 Beach Street, Coogee, NSW 2034, Australia

For information about custom editions, special sales, and premium and corporate purchases,
please contact Sterling Special Sales at 800-805-5489 or specialsales@sterlingpublishing.com.

Manufactured in China

Lot #:
2 4 6 8 10 9 7 5 3 1
10/18

sterlingpublishing.com

PHOTOGRAPHS: Alamy: © Avalon/Bruce Coleman Inc.: 21; © Avalon/Photoshot License: 3; © Chris Mattison: 25; © Morgan Trimble: 16; © Visual&Written SL: 7 left, 10; **iStock:** © ifish: 15; © Kesu01: back cover top, 2; © VictorTyakht: 14; © WhitcombeRD: 30; **Minden Pictures:** © Daniel Heuclin: 24; © Jiri Lochman: 8; © Birgitte Wilms: cover, 5, 7 right, 11; **NOAA/MBARI:** 22; **Science Source:** © Nicholas Smythe: 12; © Dr. T.E. Thompson: 26; © Melvyn Yeo: 17, back cover bottom; **Seapics.com:** © David Wrobel: 23; **Shutterstock:** © Bildagentur Zoonar GmbH: 19; © Sergio Gutierrez Getino: 20, back cover middle; © **Mariella Superina:** 13; **courtesy of Wikimedia Foundation:** Geoff Gallice: 9, 31; Sylke Rohrlach: 27; Stu's Images: 18

WEIRD Animals

BY MARY KAY CARSON

STERLING CHILDREN'S BOOKS
New York

The WHY Behind the Weird

Slime-oozing slugs, red-lipped fish, spine-covered bugs, and tubed-nosed bats. Weird animals are an awesome sight. But have you ever wondered **why**? **Why** is that slug so slimy? **Why** would a bat have such a freaky nose?

No matter how strange or wacky the animals appear, there's a reason why they look the way they do. Weird animals, like all living things, have characteristics that help them survive. An animal's color, teeth, and behavior are all adaptations that evolved over hundreds of thousands of years to help the animal find food, stay safe, and reproduce.

In this book, you'll see some fantastically weird animals! When you do, ask yourself: **Why?** Why does it look like that? How might slime or a giant nose or being blue help the animal survive? Does the curious characteristic help it hunt, find food, or hide from predators? Might the amazing adaptation warn off enemies or attract a mate?

What do YOU think?

These sentences will jump-start your brain. Each colored word matches a colored arrow that points to an explanation.

Red-Lipped Batfish

Look at those showy **red lips**! What's the giant **bump** on its head for? And where are its **fins**?

The head bump protects the small white bulb of flesh that is fake bait, like a fishing lure! When a small fish or shrimp moves in for a closer look . . . GULP! The batfish gets dinner.

Males have the reddest lips. They use them to get the attention of mates. Why red lips attract females is not known. Do you have any guesses?

These fins are made for walking, not swimming. This fish stands on its leg-like fins, waiting for prey to wander by and check out its lure.

FISHY FACTS: ANIMAL TYPE: fish • SCIENCE NAME: *Ogcocephalus darwini* SIZE: 8 inches (20 cm) long • HOME: Pacific Ocean off the coast of Peru

The colored arrows point to weird features. Think about the WHY behind the weirdness as you look. Make some guesses!

Read the explanation to find out if you were right.

Eastern Tube-Nosed Bat

What a **big-eyed** batty face! Why is its **nose** so strange?
Are these yellow **polka-dot spots** real?

This amazing nose tracks down ripe fruit. The tube-like nostrils open and close separately and also move in different directions. The bat smells in stereo!

The yellowish spots help the tube-nosed bat blend in with dry leaves to stay safe. It spends the day hanging upside down in trees.

Big eyes make it easier for this bat to find figs and other fruit it eats at night. Bats are nocturnal.

BATTY FACTS: ANIMAL TYPE: mammal • SCIENCE NAME: *Nyctimene robinsoni*
SIZE: 4 inches (10 cm) long and a wingspan of 2 ½ inches (5 cm) wide • HOME: rain forests of eastern Australia

Spiny Devil Katydid

Can you count all the **spines** on its legs and **head**?
And what might a mouth like that chomp and eat?

The head is topped with spiky thorns. It's not an easy meal for a hungry bat or another predator to swallow!

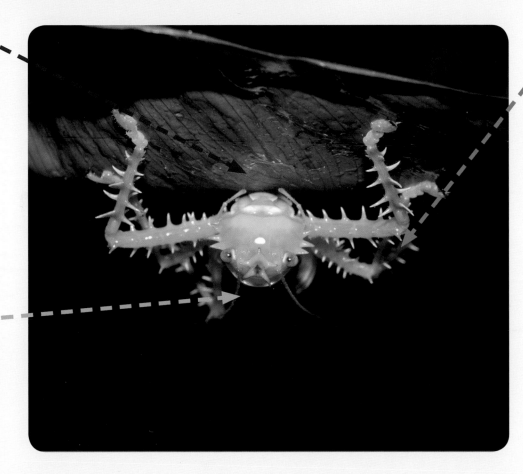

Its six spiny legs are good for fighting off enemies—and for trapping squirmy prey. During the day, the green color of this katydid helps it hide among the leafy tropical trees.

Insects don't have teeth, but this one can bite hard enough to bloody your finger! Its sharp mouth parts shred the flesh of grubs and other insects it hunts at night.

BUGGY FACTS: ANIMAL TYPE: insect • SCIENCE NAME: *Panacanthus cuspidatus*
SIZE: 2 ½ to 3 inches (6–8 cm) long • HOME: rain forests of South America

Red-Lipped Batfish

Look at those showy red lips! What's the giant **bump** on its head for? And where are its **fins**?

The head bump protects the small white bulb of flesh that is fake bait, like a fishing lure! When a small fish or shrimp moves in for a closer look . . . GULP! The batfish gets dinner.

Males have the reddest lips. They use them to get the attention of mates. Why red lips attract females is not known. Do you have any guesses?

These fins are made for walking, not swimming. This fish stands on its leg-like fins, waiting for prey to wander by and check out its lure.

FISHY FACTS: ANIMAL TYPE: fish • SCIENCE NAME: *Ogcocephalus darwini* SIZE: 8 inches (20 cm) long • HOME: Pacific Ocean off the coast of Peru

Pink Fairy Armadillo

Check out its pink **shell** and fluffy fur! Why are its feet so huge and its tail so weird?

Unlike with other armadillos, the leathery shell is loose and not connected to its backbone. But this animal still rolls into a shell-covered ball for protection. The white fur underneath keeps it warm during cold desert nights.

The tail works like a kickstand, propping up its hind end so it can shove sand and soil behind it while digging.

Oversized feet armed with giant claws power this fast digger. It can dig itself underground within seconds. The feet are also tools for tearing into underground nests of yummy ants.

PINK FAIRY FACTS: ANIMAL TYPE: mammal • SCIENCE NAME: *Chlamyphorus truncatus*
SIZE: 5 inches (13 cm) long • HOME: bushy scrubland desert of central Argentina

Saiga Antelope

Now that's a nose! Why would a grass-grazing animal need a huge, movable **snout**?
And are those candlesticks or **horns** on its head?

The waxy-looking horns are actually hard and sharp lethal weapons. Only males are armed with horns. They use them to fight over females. Why do you think the horns are wrapped in ridged rings? These bony rings help males lock horns during battle.

This gigantic nose moves this way and that—like an elephant's trunk! These fast-running antelopes migrate thousands of miles a year. Their noses keep the kicked-up dust out of their lungs. Inside the snout is a maze of snot-oozing glands, bones, and hair that filter and capture dust. During winter the big nose warms up the air the animal breathes.

NOSY FACTS: ANIMAL TYPE: mammal   •   SCIENCE NAME: *Saiga tatarica*
SIZE: 3 ¹/₂ to 5 feet (1–1.5 m) long and 2 to 2 ¹/₂ feet (0.6–0.8 m) tall at shoulder   •   HOME: dry grassland steppes of Central Asia

Peacock Mantis Shrimp

What a fruit salad of color! Are those all **legs**, or are some **arms**? Can those **eyes** move?

The amazing eyes of this mantis shrimp search out crabs, snails, and other prey. The compound eyes move on stalks and can see in all directions at the same time. They also can see more than visible light, including ultraviolet light.

These two club-tipped appendages are deadly weapons. Punching with the speed of a fired bullet, the mantis shrimp cracks open the shells of prey. When the mantis shrimp wants to scare away an unwelcome guest, it holds up its clubs and flashes the colors underneath in warning.

These three pairs of legs hold prey. The mantis shrimp walks along the seafloor with the three other leg pairs.

SMASHING FACTS: ANIMAL TYPE: crustacean • SCIENCE NAME: *Odontodactylus scyllarus*
SIZE: 2 to 7 inches (5–18 cm) long • HOME: tropical waters of the Indian and West Pacific Oceans

Shoebill

This **leggy** big bird may be taller than you! Why is its **beak** the size of a wooden shoe? And what does it do with that beak's **huge hook** anyway?

This all-business beak catches and kills big prey. It snatches 3-foot-long (92 cm) lungfish and snakes out of swamps—baby crocodiles, too! Once the prey is caught, the bird shakes its head to fling out any mud or grass from the beak. Then its sharp edges chop off the prey's head before swallowing what's left.

The big beak is also a handy bucket and scoop. Parents cool off their eggs by dumping beakfuls of water onto them. They also scoop wet grass onto the nest to keep off the sun.

There is little shade in the hot grassy swamp. Adults cool down by pooping liquid on their own legs—*ahhh*.

BIG BIRD FACTS: Animal type: bird • Science name: *Balaeniceps rex*
Size: 3 ¹/₂ to 4 ¹/₂ feet (110–140 cm) tall • Home: tropical swamps of East Africa

Mirror Spider

Did someone decorate this spider with **sequins**? What are those shiny spots on its **body**?

These pretty patches of shiny color on its body look like sequins and mirrors. But they're a kind of pigment and part of its body covering, or exoskeleton.

Not much is known about this small spider, including why it's colored like jewels. The shiny patches change shape, depending on how the spider feels. How might that help the spider survive?

SPIDEY FACTS: ANIMAL TYPE: arachnid • SCIENCE NAME: *Thwaitesia argentiopunctata*
SIZE: ¹/₈ to ¹/₆ inch (3–4 mm) long • HOME: Australia

Thorny Devil

Ouch! Why does this lizard have so many spiny thorns? And what's that big bump on its shoulders for?

Spiny thorns make this lizard a hard meal to swallow. It can also puff itself up! Its color and pattern makes perfect desert camouflage for hunting and hiding.

Morning dew collects in the deep grooves around the bottom of each spine. The grooves connect like a canal system to shuttle the water toward the mouth. This dew is often the only drinking water around.

That big bump is a "false head." When in danger, the lizard tucks its real head between its front legs and shows the fake head to the predator. Fooled ya!

SPINE-TACULAR FACTS: ANIMAL TYPE: reptile • SCIENCE NAME: *Moloch horridus*
SIZE: 4 to 8 inches (10–20 cm) long • HOME: deserts of Australia

Axolotl

Are those feathers around its **head**? Does it swim or walk? Why is its **mouth** so wide?

These aren't feathers or hairs—they're gills that take oxygen out of the water. This aquatic amphibian never leaves the water, so it breathes underwater like a fish.

The wide mouth is perfect for snapping up and sucking down worms, insects, small fish, and other aquatic prey it finds by smell.

The tail is for swimming and the feet for walking along the lake floor. It can do either! The legs and tail can also grow back if bitten off by a predator.

AXO-LENT FACTS: ANIMAL TYPE: amphibian • SCIENCE NAME: *Ambystoma mexicanum*
SIZE: 6 to 12 inches (15–30 cm) long • HOME: Mexico

Sea Pig

What is this eyeless creature? Does it even have a mouth or legs?

These squishy feet move it slowly across the floor of the deep sea. It lives as far down as $3\,^3/_4$ miles (6 km) underwater. It's a boneless invertebrate, like the tube-footed sea star and sea cucumber— cousins of the sea pig.

These longer tentacles sense food in the water. It's always dark at the lower depths, so there's no need for eyes.

Its mouth is ringed with ten short grabbing tentacles. It eats bits of whatever it can find—dead or alive, plant or animal. This one has found a crab.

PIGGY FACTS: ANIMAL TYPE: echinoderm • SCIENCE NAME: *Scotoplanes globosa*
SIZE: 4 to 6 inches (10–15 cm) long • HOME: deep ocean floor worldwide

Surinam Toad

Look more closely—that leaf has **eggs** and **feet**!
Why is it so **flat**? And are those **fingers**?

These webbed feet are for swimming, not hopping. The Surinam toad is aquatic and rarely leaves the water.

Being flat and mud-colored is perfect protection from predators. The Surinam toad can hide in plain sight from both predators and prey!

The front toes are like long, sensitive fingers that feel around for worms and small fish. They also push the prey into their wide tongueless mouth.

These babies hatch from eggs stuck onto the mom's back during mating. After months of safely surviving under mom's skin, they pop out as froglets. No tadpoles necessary!

FREAKY FACTS: ANIMAL TYPE: amphibian • SCIENCE NAME: *Pipa pipa*
SIZE: Size: 4 to 8 inches (10–20 cm) long • HOME: Amazon River in South America

Mexican Mole Lizard

Why does this lizard look like a **worm**? Why is its **head** so big and its **arms** so tiny?

It builds and lives in a maze of underground tunnels. During construction, it packs the soil of the tunnel walls by pounding it with its extra-thick skull. Meanwhile it tucks its front legs out of the way by folding them into grooves under its chest.

This odd lizard has small front legs and no back legs. The clawed feet help it burrow through sand to catch ants, grubs, worms, and bugs.

Rings of scales help move it along like an earthworm. Inside the tunnels, it scoots forward and backward by squeezing the muscles in its long body.

FIVE-TOED FACTS: ANIMAL TYPE: reptile • SCIENCE NAME: *Bipes biporus*
SIZE: 7 1/2 to 9 inches (18–22 cm) long • HOME: sandy deserts of Baja, Mexico

Blue Dragon Sea Slug

Why is this deadly sea creature blue on top and **gray** below? Is it swimming or just **floating**? Are those fins or **fingers**?

This air bubble in its belly keeps it afloat, like a pool floaty. Its bright blue topside blends in with the water and waves, camouflaging it from hungry seabirds overhead.

Its underside is silvery gray, so it almost disappears from view when a predator swimming below looks up toward the shiny sea surface.

Watch out! These finger-like appendages pack a powerful sting. The stingers are from venomous jellyfish it ate. The swallowed stingers became part of the slug's body. It swims toward prey or mates by moving the appendages, too.

SEA SLUG FACTS: ANIMAL TYPE: mollusk • SCIENCE NAME: *Glaucus atlanticus*
SIZE: up to 1 ¼ inch (3 cm) long • HOME: temperate and tropical oceans worldwide

WEIRD WORDS TO KNOW

amphibian – an animal that lives on both land and water—such as a frog, toad, or salamander

appendage – a body part like an arm, leg, or tentacle that's connected to the main body

aquatic – living in water

arachnid – an invertebrate animal with eight legs—such as a spider, scorpion, tick, or mite

echinoderm – sea-living invertebrate animal—such as a sea star (starfish), sea cucumber, or sea urchin

crustacean – an invertebrate animal with many-jointed legs and a hard exoskeleton—such as a lobster, shrimp, barnacle, or pillbug

exoskeleton – the outer covering, or shell, of many invertebrates

invertebrate – an animal without a backbone

mammal – a warm-blooded vertebrate animal that gives birth to live young and has fur or hair—such as a dog, rat, human, or whale

mollusk – an invertebrate animal with a soft body and usually a shell—such as a slug, snail, clam, or octopus

nocturnal - active at night

predator – an animal that hunts and eats other animals

reptile – a cold-blooded vertebrate animal that lays eggs and that has a body covered with scales—such as a snake, lizard, or turtle

(in) stereo - sounds, smells, or sights coming from two different directions

tentacle – an invertebrate animal's long flexible arm

venomous – capable of injecting poison with a sting or bite

vertebrate – an animal with a backbone

INDEX